Thank you for purchasing my book!

My name is Mirabelle, I'm an indie author and a full time parent.
I've been working on creating fun and educational games, stories and books for kids for the past 12 years.

As a parent of two, finding ways to entertain the kids while teaching them how to think, communicate and learn important values has been one of my top priorities.
Developing curiosity and creative imagination has become crucial to adapt and grow in today's society.

I really hope you enjoy this book, and if you do, please consider leaving us a review sharing your experience, I'd love to read it and I'd really appreciate it!

'Laughter is timeless, imagination has no age and dreams are forever' - Walt Disney

A child's imagination knows no boundaries. Children have an innate ability to imagine and create stories from scratch and are always looking for new ideas and experiences to understand the world around them.

These "Would You Rather? - Ridiculousness Edition" questions will stimulate your kids' imagination and bring out some amazingly insightful, funny and interesting answers.

This book is a great tool to :

• **Improve communication** by encouraging your children to talk and express themselves freely while discussing their choices in a fun and light-hearted way.

• **Encourage critical thinking** : these questions will help children develop hypotheses about the different scenarios and encourage them to think in new and different ways.

• **Stimulate imagination and creative thinking** through our list of ridiculous and original scenarios.

• **Strengthen relationships** by spurring healthy and interactive discussion in a fun and care-free environment.

• **Nurture curiosity and improve general knowledge** with our list of unique and quite "random" facts.

These questions are an excellent idea to get the conversation started!

Meet Twinkles!

He's an adorable and loveable friend with a big tall hat,
he is short and likes to cuddle with his affectionate cat.
He always wears a funny red noise,
and you cannot help but notice his very pointy toes.
Twinkles makes a sad day wonderfully mellow,
he will sing you a song while playing the cello.
Despite his age, he is really wise,
and with his tricks and pranks, it's always a happy surprise.

Welcome to Twinkles' adventurous world !

How to Play ?

- *Play with minimum two players : Choose at least one other player besides yourself to play the game. If you have a large group of people, you can play around in a circle or even form teams.*

- *Choose the first player who will ask a question that begins with "Would you rather...?" and provide the two scenarios for the second player to choose from.*

- *The second player has to choose **only one scenario** – without revealing their choice.*

- *Now, the first player will have to guess which answer the second player has chosen. If their guess is correct, they score one point*

- *The second player will have **to explain their choice** !*

- *Make sure to keep scores and decide on a prize or a challenge for each round !*

Most importantly, have fun, laugh and enjoy your time with your family and loved ones!

Round 1

WOULD YOU RATHER ?

have butterfly wings
or...
a horse tail?

eat onion-flavored
cookies
or..
chicken-flavored ice cream?

WOULD YOU RATHER ?

*burp every time
you wink
or...
fart every time you laugh?*

*put your foot into a sock
full of worms
or...
into a sock full of itchy
powder?*

WOULD YOU RATHER ?

have to do a silly dance every time you say "hi"
or...
run in a circle three times when you say "bye"?

be able to change the color of your hair whenever you want
or...
be able to change the length of your hair whenever you want?

WOULD YOU RATHER ?

*be covered in sticky honey
or...
be covered in melted
marshmallows?*

*eat a whole raw potato
or...
a lemon ?*

WOULD YOU RATHER ?

stick your finger in a
giraffe's nose
or...
in an elephant's ear?

visit the moon once
or...
live in your favorite place
for the rest of your life ?

Did You Know...?

- Scientists estimate that there are between 15000 and 20000 different species of butterfly.

- A burp is just a lot of hot air! When you're eating food or drinking a beverage, you're not just swallowing your food and drink, you're also swallowing air!

- Raw potatoes are more likely to clash with your digestive system and may contain more antinutrients and harmful compounds.

- A spacecraft takes about 3 days to reach the Moon. The distance traveled is around 240,000 miles (386,400 kilometers).

Round 2

WOULD YOU RATHER ?

be sprayed with silly string all over your body or... have a pie smashed onto your face?

be chased by hundreds of angry bees or... get trapped in a cave with ten smelly skunks?

WOULD YOU RATHER ?

fart clouds of dust
or...
sneeze out spaghetti?

turn into a frog for a day
once a week
or...
a random animal for 2
hours everyday?

WOULD YOU RATHER ?

> *brush your teeth with
> lemon juice
> or...
> take a ginger bath?*

> *become a grown up
> tomorrow
> or...
> stay the age you are
> now for 10 years?*

WOULD YOU RATHER ?

have a flying magic
carpet
or...
an all-glass submarine?

hug everyone in
the room for 5 minutes
or...
go outside and hug
a tree for 10 minutes?

WOULD YOU RATHER ?

> *lick the wall
> or...
> put hot sauce on
> ice cream and eat it?*

> *be incredibly lucky
> or...
> incredibly smart?*

Did You Know...?

- Bees have 5 eyes and 6 legs.
- Male bees in the hive are called drones and they do not have a stinger.
- Worker bees are females. They do all the different tasks needed to operate and maintain the hive.

- Frogs drink water through their skin

- Farts are also caused when bacteria in the stomach produces gas as the food we eat is broken down.
- In one day, you pass enough gas to fill a balloon!
- Most people fart about 14 times a day. ...

Round 3

WOULD YOU RATHER ?

*fall of your bicycle
or...
hit in the face by a ball?*

*only be able to run on
a potato sack
or...
only be able to move
riding a unicycle?*

WOULD YOU RATHER ?

live in the jungle
or...
in the North Pole?

have the power to
create fire
or...
water?

WOULD YOU RATHER ?

own a giant robot
or...
flying boat?

have spiders crawl on you
or...
be chased by an angry
hippo?

WOULD YOU RATHER ?

*kiss a frog
or...
sleep with a pig?*

*have a giraffe neck
or...
an elephant trunk?*

WOULD YOU RATHER ?

have all of your hair cut off
or...
lose five teeth?

stand on Lego
or...
be pricked by a needle?

Did You Know...?

- *Hippopotamuses are mammals and are the third largest land animal. They live most of their life in water, and can be found in Africa*

- *Giraffes are the tallest mammals on Earth.*
- *A giraffe's neck is too short to reach the ground.*
- *Giraffes only need to drink once every few days.*

- *Spiders are not insects.*
- *Most spiders are not dangerous to humans.*
- *The wolf spider carries her babies on her back with her.*

Round 4

WOULD YOU RATHER ?

be able to do magic
or...
be the funniest kid in
school?

cry 7 times a week
or...
laugh for six hours
every day?

WOULD YOU RATHER ?

get your favorite toy
or...
be your favorite superhero?

have tea with an angry
bear
or...
a hungry tiger?

WOULD YOU RATHER ?

*eat mud
or...
lick the bottom of your
shoes at the end of a day?*

*live in the forest only
eating vegetables
or...
near the ocean only eating
fish?*

WOULD YOU RATHER ?

have ears as small as a mouse
or...
a nose like a hammerhead shark?

have a head filled with air
or...
a body made of blanket fleece?

WOULD YOU RATHER ?

be a bird that barks
or...
a dolphin that oinks?

get stuck in sinking sand
or...
never be able to get off a
swing?

Did You Know...?

- *Dolphins are extremely intelligent animals. They live up to 50 years!*
- *When they're asleep, one part of their brains remain awake and alert.*
- *Baby hammerheads are called pups.*
- *A hammerhead mom can give birth to up to 50 babies at once.*
- *Similar to humans, a female shark is pregnant for about 8 to 10 months.*
- *Tigers can sprint at over 60 kilometre/hour.*
- *Tigers urine smells like buttered popcorn.*

Round 5

WOULD YOU RATHER ?

> *have hands that cannot*
> *hold onto objects*
> *or...*
> *legs that can only run?*

> *have a magic closet that gave*
> *you new clothes every day*
> *or...*
> *a magic book that completed*
> *your homework for you every*
> *day?*

WOULD YOU RATHER ?

eat spinach flavoured lollipops
or...
eat ice cream flavoured soup with vegetables inside?

have belly button in your forehead
or...
a belly button in your chin?

WOULD YOU RATHER ?

have toys that could come alive
or...
an endless supply of sweets?

walk sideways like a crab forever
or...
jump like a grasshopper forever?

WOULD YOU RATHER ?

beep like a truck every time you walk backwards

or...

pretend to fly every time you see an airplane?

have the ability to see from a very far distance

or...

be able to ride dolphins?

WOULD YOU RATHER ?

have the power to detect lies

or...

have the ability to make others believe whatever you say?

find a pirate treasure map

or...

travel to the end of a rainbow?

Did You Know...?

- *Rainbows are made up of seven colors: red, orange, yellow, green, blue, indigo, and violet.*
- *On the ground, we can only see a semi-circle rainbow but if you look at it from an airplane, you can see a rainbow in a complete circle.*
- *Earth is the only planet in the solar system where rainbows are possible.*
- *The first lie detector instrument was invented in 1906 by Sir James McKenzie (a cardiologist).*
- *Grasshoppers have ears on their bellies.`*
- *In many countries, grasshoppers are considered a delicate food.*

Round 6

WOULD YOU RATHER ?

have everyday be your birthday
or...
Christmas?

be able to glow in the dark
or...
have a beam of light shoot from your hand like a torch?

WOULD YOU RATHER ?

have a crime-solving dog that can talk to you with their mind

or...

a talking dog that sees the future but doesn't tell you about your future?

enter the cage of a sleeping lion for 20 minutes

or...

swim across a river infested with crocodiles?

WOULD YOU RATHER ?

have a secret robot that cleans up your room for you
or...
a secret robot that does all your homework?

go on the world's tallest roller coaster but it moves really slowly
or...
the world's longest water slide but it's filled with jello?

WOULD YOU RATHER ?

PLAYER 1

have a magic wand that turns every third spell into a random one

or...

a flying broom that flies with the speed of a turtle?

PLAYER 2

have to repeat everything you say twice

or...

have to scream what you say otherwise people can't hear you?

WOULD YOU RATHER ?

that dragons be real but the sizes of dogs
or...
that dogs were the size of dragons?

take only cold showers for a month
or...
sleep under the rain for a week?

- *No one really knows where the legends and stories of dragons came from or started.*
- *Some dragons are said to blow fire, other dragons fly, some blow ice*
- *The world's tallest water slide measures 1,111 meters (3,645 feet) long and could be found in the country of Malaysia.*
- *Spending 16-20 hours of the day sleeping or resting, lions are the laziest of the big cats.*
- *Crocodiles have the strongest bite of any animal in the world.*
- *The saltwater crocodile is the largest species of crocodile.*

Round 7

WOULD YOU RATHER ?

*earn $100 after washing
the dishes for a week
or...
be given $50 after
changing 3 baby diapers?*

*be a knight who can't ride
a horse
or...
be a pirate who always
gets seasick?*

WOULD YOU RATHER ?

*have fingernails that grow
1 inch every day
or...
have no fingernails at all?*

*never have to brush your
teeth again
or...
never have to wash your
face again?*

WOULD YOU RATHER ?

stay at school two more hours every day
or...
have to go to school on Saturdays?

have to wear your pants backwards
or...
shoes on the wrong feet?

WOULD YOU RATHER ?

> *have a monkey's tail that you can't use to climb*
> *or...*
> *rabbit's ears that make your hearing worse?*

> *be the most powerful wizard*
> *or...*
> *the weakest superhero?*

WOULD YOU RATHER ?

have to go to school wearing a clown wig or... a clown nose?

have an giraffe-sized rabbit or... a rabbit-sized bear?

Did You Know...?

- *A baby rabbit is called a kit, a female is called a doe and a male is called a buck.*
- *A rabbit's teeth never stop growing!*

- *There are around 260 monkey species in the world. Most of them live in trees except for a few who seem to prefer the ground like baboons.*

- *Fingernails grow about 2 times faster than toenails.*
- *They grow faster in summer than winter.*
- *It doesn't hurt to cut your nails because the nail is dead.*

Round 8

WOULD YOU RATHER ?

> *eat a spoonful of mustard*
> *or...*
> *a raw egg?*

> *eat a fried cricket*
> *or...*
> *a fried grasshopper sandwich?*

WOULD YOU RATHER ?

get all the year's presents at one time and nothing special on your birthday

or...

get one present a month with a single extra present for Christmas?

be able to talk to cats

or...

dogs?

WOULD YOU RATHER ?

be in a tank with a shark
you can ride
or...
an electric eel that you can
pet?

eat an entire plate of
burnt-black pizza
or...
eat an entire head of
broccoli?

WOULD YOU RATHER ?

*have antennas like an ant
or...
the legs of a frog?*

*be able to roar like
a lion
or...
sing like a bird?*

WOULD YOU RATHER ?

PLAYER 1

*get tickled for 2 minutes
or...
take a shower with
your clothes on?*

PLAYER 2

*give up summer vacation but
get perfect grades and
graduate early
or...
have a break that lasts half
the year but go to school 24/7
the other half of the year?*

Did You Know...?

- *You Can't Tickle Yourself ! Why not? - Essentially, we cannot surprise our own brain. Our brains are programmed to evade anticipated stimuli, including - perhaps most tellingly - tactile perceptions resulting from our own movements.*

- *An ant can lift 20 times its own body weight.*

- *Ants use antennae to notice scents in the air, touch other ants, tap the ground, and check out pieces of food.*

- *The Loudest Roar: A male lion has the loudest roar of any big cats species, it can be heard from up to five miles away.*

Round 9

WOULD YOU RATHER ?

PLAYER 1

get a really bad sunburn that lasts for months whilst on the best vacation of your life

or...

not get hurt at all but it is the most boring holiday ever?

PLAYER 2

have the ability to make people dance every time you sneeze

or...

rolling on the floor every time you clap?

WOULD YOU RATHER ?

PLAYER 1

have thick hair on the backs of your hands like a monkey
or...
have grasping monkey feet that won't fit in any shoes?

PLAYER 2

own a talking gorilla
or...
have an alien be your best friend?

WOULD YOU RATHER ?

*have smelly farts every five minutes that are silent
or...
have super loud, but not stinky, farts every hour?*

*climb a mountain wearing your slippers
or...
walk on ice barefoot?*

WOULD YOU RATHER ?

never get sick again because you only eat brussels sprouts
or...
eat only pizza but be sick once every day?

jump every time you drink a glass of water
or...
spin in circles for 30 seconds ?

WOULD YOU RATHER ?

become famous because you have the world's oiliest skin

or...

become rich but can only shop at pound/dollar stores?

live in a house built from marshmallows

or...

a house built from candy?

Did You Know...?

- *Candy is simply made by dissolving sugar in water.*
- *Chew gum until the sugar is gone to blow a bigger bubble. Sugar does not stretch and can cause the bubble to collapse early.*
- *The largest organ in your body, skin is just a few millimeters thick. Your skin is waterproof, keeps out germs, and repairs itself.*
- *How did pizza get its name? Pizza could come from the Greek word "pitta" meaning "pie", or the Langobardic word "bizzo" meaning "bite".*

Round 10

WOULD YOU RATHER ?

PLAYER 1

> *eat your favourite breakfast food every morning but it makes you throw up an hour later*
> *or...*
> *eat kale every night for dessert?*

PLAYER 2

> *have bright green hair*
> *or...*
> *a banana sized earrings?*

WOULD YOU RATHER ?

PLAYER 1

spend the night alone
in a haunted house
or...
be chased by a zombie?

PLAYER 2

get top marks in your year but
never play your favourite video
game again
or...
fail two classes a year but
have one class dedicated to
playing that video game?

WOULD YOU RATHER ?

*always talk and act
like a robot
or...
have your finger always
stuck into your nose?*

*travel back in time to see
dinosaurs but no one believes you
or...
travel forward in time to see a
colonized Mars and then that's all
anyone ever talks to you about
for the rest of your life?*

WOULD YOU RATHER ?

> *live next door to your best friend but can only talk with them at school*
> *or...*
> *you can only talk to your best friend through text?*

> *eat a whole jar of mayonnaise*
> *or...*
> *drink a cup of hot sauce?*

WOULD YOU RATHER ?

PLAYER 1

*wash your face with toilet water every day for a week
or...
you fall out of bed every morning for a week?*

PLAYER 2

*have half the meals you eat in a week be the foods you hate the most
or...
have all deserts taste like tuna?*

Did You Know...?

- *Tuna are a streamlined silver fish with large eyes, dark blue backs and spiky fins. Tuna are normally between 1-2m in length.*

- *Mayonnaise (also known as Mayo) is a thick sauce. It is a combination of vegetable oil and egg yolk, with either lemon juice or vinegar.*

- *There were actually reptiles on Earth before dinosaurs. Before the first first dinosaurs walked the Earth about 230 million years ago, the earth was dominated by reptiles known as archosaurs and therapsids.*

Round 11

WOULD YOU RATHER ?

flip yourself upside down and walk on your hands whenever you hear a car honk

or...

go onto all fours and walk like a crab when you hear someone whistle?

eat a small can of dog food

or...

eat three rotten tomatoes?

WOULD YOU RATHER ?

*have a monkey face
or...
a pig nose?*

*be the sidekick of a mad
scientist who tests new
inventions on you
or...
the sidekick a supervillain
who is always being thrown
in jail?*

WOULD YOU RATHER ?

be able to explore space but you're in charge of cleaning the toilets

or...

be in a submarine at the bottom of the ocean with a crew that gets sea-sick?

sneeze ice cream

or...

have your tears be candy flavored?

WOULD YOU RATHER ?

*eat two tablespoons
full of liquid soap
or...
drink a glass full of
salty water?*

*have a cool new shirt every
morning
or...
have a new pair of shoes
every morning?*

WOULD YOU RATHER ?

have 500 grasshoppers in the rest of the house
or...
100 spiders in your bedroom?

be eating your cereal only to realize that the milk is sour
or...
take a bite out of a rotten hard-boiled egg?

Did You Know...?

- *Pigs have a keen sense of smell detecting food deep into ground roots with their very sensitive nose.*

- *Grasshoppers have six legs, a pair of antennas, four wings and small little pinchers to cut food which typically consists of grasses, leaves.*

- *If we drink salty water to quench our thirst, the kidneys have to use existing water from our body in order to dilute the extra salt, which in turn makes us feel even thirstier*

- *Our tears actually taste salty because they contain natural salts called electrolytes.*

Round 12

WOULD YOU RATHER ?

make fire from your hands but only the size of a small candle's flame

or...

control water in the form of dewdrops?

be able to play video games using only your mind

or...

be able to eat without using your hands?

WOULD YOU RATHER ?

be turned into a rat for a week
or...
have to live with a rat as big as you are for a week?

have to use a public toilet that has a snake in it
or...
one that it is dark and extremely dirty?

WOULD YOU RATHER ?

have to blend up all your food and drink it

or...

have everything you drink be a solid that you have to eat?

start dancing every time you sneeze

or...

rolling on the floor every time you fart?

WOULD YOU RATHER ?

only be able to wear your swimsuit for the rest of your life
or...
only be able to wear pants and a winter coat?

meet an alien
or...
meet a dinosaur?

WOULD YOU RATHER ?

> *never have to shower again*
> *or...*
> *never have to brush your teeth again?*

> *be super tall with your neck being the longest part of your body*
> *or...*
> *very short because your head rests on top of your legs?*

Did You Know...?

- *Our bodies are mostly water. A newborn baby is 78 percent water.*
- *Most freshwater on our planet is in ice.*
- *A fire needs fuel, oxygen, and heat to burn.*
- *Flames are the visible part of a fire. Their color depends on the fuel.*
- *Fire causes severe burns and blisters on humans*
- *A sneeze can travel up to 100 mph. (160km/hour)*
- *Rats' super-strong teeth never stop growing!*

Round 13

WOULD YOU RATHER ?

walk over a rainbow
or...
ride a shooting star?

raise lowing (mooing)
chickens
or...
raise clucking cows?

WOULD YOU RATHER ?

PLAYER 1

talk and laugh like Goofy whenever you're trying to be serious
or...
talk like Donald Duck when you are sad?

PLAYER 2

be stuck in a hole full of spiders
or...
be stuck up a tree draped in snakes?

WOULD YOU RATHER ?

have a superhuman memory
or...
be able to write super fast?

be bitten by 30
mosquitoes
or...
be stung by a bee
7 times?

WOULD YOU RATHER ?

be stuck on a boat in the middle of the ocean
or...
a space rocket floating in space?

discover a hidden treasure
or...
discover a living dinosaur?

WOULD YOU RATHER ?

get caught sneaking out of your house
or...
get caught eating candy before bed?

be able to speak 7 different languages
or...
memorize the lyrics of every single song you hear?

Did You Know...?

- *Shooting stars are not actually stars! They are small rocks and dust penetrating the Earth's upper atmosphere at extremely high speeds.*

- *A "moonbow" is a lunar rainbow, an astonishing and rare phenomenon that can only occur at night under very specific conditions.*

- *Mosquitoes are a small, flying insect, with many species that feed on blood from a live host.*

- *Female mosquitoes that do feed on blood prefer a specific host.*

Round 14

WOULD YOU RATHER ?

*throw confetti on everyone
you meet for a week
or ...
blow a horn every time
you meet someone?*

*not be able to talk
ever again
or...
only be able to yell
when you speak?*

WOULD YOU RATHER ?

be able to speak to animals
or...
speak every single
human language?

have a puppy that always
pees when it sees you
or...
a kitten that bites your
pinky toe?

WOULD YOU RATHER ?

PLAYER 1

be able to climb and swing from webs like Spider-Man but the web comes from your bum

or...

have claws like Wolverine but they are made of spaghetti noodles?

PLAYER 2

eat three spiders

or...

eat a bowl full of worms?

WOULD YOU RATHER ?

> *constantly itch*
> *or...*
> *always have a cough?*

> *become the size of*
> *dinosaur*
> *or...*
> *be shrunk down to the*
> *size of a bug?*

WOULD YOU RATHER ?

> be trapped in the boot of a car for one night
> or...
> trapped in a lift for an entire day?

> lose your sense of smell forever
> or...
> lose your sense of taste forever?

Did You Know...?

- *The sauropods were the largest and heaviest dinosaurs, reaching a length of 30 meters (98 ft.) and a weight of 88 tons.*

- *Taste is one of the five senses. It is the sensation that a human or animal experiences on the tongue when eating. Usually, there are the tastes of sweet, sour, bitter, spicy, and salty*

- *Smell is the first sense babies use after they are born. Until the age of 4, all smells are never gross, only interesting.*

Final Round

WOULD YOU RATHER ?

learn how to sword fight with a swordfish
or...
be taught how to box from a kangaroo?

go to a museum and be able to touch everything
or...
an aquarium and swim with the fish?

WOULD YOU RATHER ?

be friends with superman
or...
spiderman?

say out loud everything
that comes to your mind
or...
lose the ability to speak
unless someone spoke to
you?

WOULD YOU RATHER ?

drive a truck that plays "This is the Song that Never Ends" whenever it moves

or...

ride on a motorcycle that leaves a trail of glitter and rainbows wherever it goes?

get a $50 allowance every week but you have to clean the toilet every day

or...

get straight A's but have to stay behind in class to scrape gum off the floor?

WOULD YOU RATHER ?

*be able to talk without
moving your lips
or...
see with your eyes closed?*

*get wrapped from head to
toe in toilet paper
or...
put ice cubes down your
shirt with your shirt
tucked in?*

WOULD YOU RATHER ?

own an old-timey pirate
ship and crew
or...
a private jet with a pilot
and infinite fuel?

to jump as far as a
kangaroo
or...
hold your breath as long
as a whale?

Did You Know...?

- *Kangaroos come from a family of animals called macropods, which means 'large foot'.*
- *Kangaroos' bodies are designed for jumping! They have short front legs, powerful back legs, huge back feet and strong tails. All of these help them to jump around and their tail balances them.*
- *Whales breathe air as we do. To breathe, whales have a blowhole in the top of their heads.*
- *The largest animals to have ever lived on Earth, blue whales can grow to over 30m long and weigh more than 130,000kg — that's longer than three buses and heavier than three lorries!*

Congratulations !

You succeeded at this ridiculous decision making challenge !

I hope you had a fun time reading the book. If you enjoyed it, I would really appreciate if you leave us a review sharing your experience and stories. **It would mean a lot !!**

If you haven't done so already, make sure to check out my other books and follow my author's page on Amazon for future releases !

Till next time,
Mirabelle <3

Riddle Quest
BONUS ACCESS

Join our fun club and get bonus monthly access to our giveaways & extras !

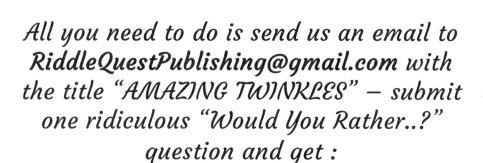

All you need to do is send us an email to *RiddleQuestPublishing@gmail.com* with the title *"AMAZING TWINKLES"* — submit one ridiculous *"Would You Rather..?"* question and get :

- An entry to our monthly giveaway to win **50$ Amazon Gift Card** !

- Access to our **free extras** !

A winner with the best submission will be picked each month and will be contacted via email.

Best of Luck !